How a Library Works

by Amanda StJohn

illustrated by
Bob Ostrom

The Child's World®

Published by The Child's World®
1980 Lookout Drive • Mankato, MN 56003-1705
800-599-READ • www.childsworld.com

Acknowledgments
The Child's World®: Mary Berendes, Publishing Director
The Design Lab: Design and production
Red Line Editorial: Editorial direction

ISBN 9781614732471
LCCN 2012932866

Printed in the United States of America
Mankato, MN
July 2012
PA02127

About the Author

Amanda StJohn is an author and public librarian.
She's fascinated by singing frogs and animal tracks
and enjoys apricot tea and knitting.

About the Illustrator

Bob Ostrom is an award-winning children's
illustrator. His work has been featured in
more than two hundred children's books and
publications. When Bob is not illustrating children's
books you can usually find him in a classroom or
online teaching kids how to draw.

The little town of O'Hare had the O'Hare Public Library. To Stew Rabbit, the public library looked as big as an elephant—maybe as big as six elephants!

Inside, there were tables and soft chairs. There were bookshelves lined up as far as Stew could see. "Wow," sighed Stew.

Stew had never been to the O'Hare library before. His eyes were as big as cabbages as he looked around. "Whoops!" He bumped into an owl.

"Cool bag!" piped Stew. "I mean, I'm sorry. I'm Stew."

The owl giggled. "I'm Opal. You must be new." Stew nodded shyly.

"That's cool," said Opal. "Let me show you how this place works."

Opal and Stew went to the front of the library. "Here's the checkout desk," she pointed. "You can get a library card here. You can return books that you read, and you can check out, or borrow, new books."

"Awesome," replied Stew.

"No," Opal retorted. She pointed at a computer station nearby. "*This* is awesome. It's a self-checkout station. You can use your library card to borrow books all by yourself."

Beyond the self-checkout station, Stew saw a young mouse clap with excitement. Her grandmother was nodding her head yes.

"What's happening over there?" Stew asked.

Opal led the way. "This," she said," is where the library keeps movies."

"Look at all those DVDs!" Stew dashed to a special rack. "And video games!"

"Careful, Stew," whispered Opal. "We don't run in the library. We walk."

Stew snapped his fingers. "Got it."

"With your library card, you can borrow any of these items."

"Wow!" Stew shook his head with amazement.

Suddenly, Stew had a thought. If a library shares movies and video games, it must also share music.

"If you like music," Opal waved her hand, "Come see what's over here."

Shelves loaded with CDs surrounded Opal and Stew. There were more CDs in the middle of the room.

"Those on the wall," pointed Opal, "are audiobooks, or books read on CD."

Stew nodded to the CDs in the middle of the room. "What are those, then?"

"Music," smiled Opal.

"Nooooo waaaaay!" shouted Stew.

"Shhh!" cautioned Opal. "Use your library voice."

Stew was confused. "Library voice?"

Opal explained that using one's library voice meant speaking in a soft whisper. "Many people come here to study," she explained. "Look behind you."

Stew turned around. He saw magazines and newspapers. At a table, some young lizards were working on homework. Other folks were reading books. Suddenly, Stew wanted a book to read, too.

Stew saw a long line of shelves bursting with books. "Let's pick a storybook, Opal."

In a flash, he zoomed away.

"Wait!" Opal gasped, but Stew didn't hear.

"Whoops!" Ms. Mantis put up her hand. "Stop, please."

Errrrrt! Stew came to a halt. He bent over to catch his breath.

"I'm Ms. Mantis, the children's librarian," she said. "We don't run in the library."

Stew's ears drooped. "Sorry," he said. "I forgot. I saw these stories. May I read one?"

By then, Opal caught up. "Stew, I was trying to tell you that these books are for adults."

"Huh?" Stew scratched his head. He looked at the shelf and saw large, thick books.

"Aren't there any for kids?" he worried.

Ms. Mantis smiled. "The library is set up in sections, Stew. There is a section for adults, a section for teens . . ."

"And a place just for kids?" Stew finished.

"Definitely," nodded Ms. Mantis.

Opal and Stew walked with Ms. Mantis to the children's room. Fish swam in a tank. A young bear shared pretend tea with a stuffed unicorn.

"You can play games and toys here, or check them out for awhile," grinned Opal.

"Cool place!" blurted Stew.

"I know, right?" Opal sighed.

Stew found computers and **tablets**. Ms. Mantis showed Stew how to sign up to use them. He could play with them for thirty minutes if he wanted. Then he had to share with the next person.

"Story hour!" sang Ms. Mantis.

Stew's ears perked up. "Stories?"

Children gathered around Ms. Mantis. Opal and Stew went, too. They sang songs. Ms. Mantis read stories aloud. Stew laughed when Ms. Mantis pretended to be a mouse eating cheese. At the end of story hour, Ms. Mantis helped everyone make a mouse mask to wear.

"Opal," Stew whispered. "That was so much fun. I wish it didn't have to end."

"Don't worry," chuckled Opal. "Ms. Mantis does story hour every week."

Opal told Stew about other **programs** the library had for kids. Stew could come learn sign language, or get help with his homework—all at the library.

Then, Opal said, "Let's read a story, Stew."

Stew slipped a book off a shelf. "This one?"

Opal giggled, "Sure! But that's not a story book."

Stew looked at his hands. He was holding a how-to-draw-dinosaurs book.

"This is the **nonfiction** section," Opal pointed out. "That means not make-believe."

A few steps away, Opal and Stew found a section marked "**Fiction**."

"Oh, here are the storybooks," Stew declared.

A worker rolled a cart of books past Opal and Stew.

"That's Joey," she said. "Joey is a page—that means he puts books back on the shelf."

"How does he know where they all go?" Stew wondered.

"Hmm," said Opal. "I forget. Let's ask someone."

18

Opal took Stew to Ms. Mantis's desk. "Come here if you ever have a question."

"Hi again," said Ms. Mantis. "May I help you?"

"How does Joey know where those books go?" asked Opal.

Ms. Mantis thought this was an excellent question. "He reads the call numbers. Every book has a call number on its spine. The number tells where the book belongs. Here, I'll show you."

From a cart nearby, Ms. Mantis picked up two children's books. "Which one of these is fiction?"

"The storybook about a princess is fiction," answered Opal.

"Fantastic!" said Ms. Mantis. "All fiction books are shelved in alphabet order by the author's last name."

"This author's last name is Higgins," Stew tried. "So the call number says H-i-g for Higgins."

"Exact-a-mundo!" quipped Ms. Mantis.

"What about the other book?" Stew wondered.

Opal pointed. "It's nonfiction—not fake."

"Nonfiction call numbers have numbers and letters. This book is 796.3 B-l-o," said the librarian.

Opal asked, "What's with the numbers?"

"They're part of the Dewey Decimal system. It groups books by subject," explained Ms. Mantis.

"I don't get it yet," groaned Opal.

"Books marked 796 will be about soccer or other sports. Books marked 636 will be about dogs and other pets. The library **catalog** will tell you what call number your book has so you can find it."

"Got it," nodded Opal.

"What about the letters?" Stew pressed.

"The letters tell us the author's last name. That helps us put all the dog books or all the soccer books in order."

"Clever!" grinned Stew.

Stew looked around the children's library. "I like the library."

"There's always something new to learn," declared Opal.

Opal and Stew shook Ms. Mantis's hand and said goodbye. After such a long day of excitement, they were quite hungry. Stew's tummy grumbled aloud.

"Want to share a snack with me, Stew?" Opal held out a sweet apple.

"That's a big YES!" Stew took the apple and nearly bit into it.

Opal whispered, "Wait! We don't eat inside the library."

"Oh," Stew giggled. "Got it."

From that day forward, Opal and Stew were the best of friends. They visited O'Hare Public Library together often. And every time they visited the library, they learned something new.

Glossary

catalog (KAT-uh-lawg): The catalog is the complete list of items a library has to offer. Stew and Opal searched the catalog for books to read.

fiction (FIK-shun): Fiction stories are stories about characters and events that are not real. Stew liked fiction books about rabbits.

nonfiction (NON-fik-shun): Nonfiction writings tell real facts about the world. Opal liked nonfiction books about mummies.

programs (PROH-grams): Programs are classes and events for you to attend at the library. Opal and Stew went to a library program to learn sign language.

tablets (TAB-lits): Tablets are small, computer-like devices for playing games or reading eBooks. Stew saw people using tablets at the library.

Tips to Remember!

- Walk, don't run.
- Shhh, use your library voice.
- No food or drinks in the library, please.
- Get to know your children's librarian.
- Ask for help when you need it.

Web Sites

Visit our Web site for links about library skills: childsworld.com/links

Note to Parents, Teachers, and Librarians: We routinely verify our Web links to make sure they are safe and active sites. So encourage your readers to check them out!

Books

Enderle, Dotti. *The Library Gingerbread Man.* Janesville, WI: Upstart Books, 2010.

Fertig, Dennis. *Chester Visits the Library.* New York: Scholastic, 2011.

Rey, Margaret, and H. A. Rey. *Curious George Visits the Library.* Boston: Houghton Mifflin, 2003.